D1750037

See the USA

NEW YORK
NEW YORK

by
Paul J. Deegan

CRESTWOOD HOUSE
New York

LIBRARY OF CONGRESS CATALOGING IN PUBLICATION DATA

Deegan, Paul J., 1937-
  New York, New York / by Paul J. Deegan : edited by Marion Dane Bauer.

  p. cm. — (See the USA)
  Includes index.
  SUMMARY: A tour of New York City from lower Manhattan and the Statue of Liberty through midtown and Fifth Avenue to uptown Central Park and Harlem. Includes facts about the city, an area map, and where to write for more information.
  1. New York (N.Y.)—Description—1981—Juvenile literature. 2. Manhattan (New York, N.Y.)—Description—Juvenile literature. [1. New York (N.Y.)—Description. 2. Manhattan (New York, N.Y.)—Description.] I. Bauer, Marion Dane. II. Title. III. Series.
F128.33.D44   1989   917.47'10443—dc20   89-32945
ISBN 0-89686-467-7   CIP
                                                        AC

PHOTO CREDITS

Cover: Peter Arnold, Inc.: Walker
Peter Arnold, Inc.: (Thomas Laird) 4, 14; (Malcolm S. Kirk) 6; (Cecile Brunswick) 11, 20, 27; (Walker) 12, 26; (Bruno J. Zehnder) 15, 16, 29, 42; (Eduardo Bermudez) 18; (Laura Dwight) 19, 23; (Carol Kitman) 22; (Dan Porges) 24; (C. O. Slavens) 32; (James H. Karales) 40
Third Coast Stock Source: (R. Lee) 9; (Jeff Lowe) 13; (James R. Peterson) 30; (Brian Yarvin) 31; (James A. Klingbeil) 34; (Eric Oxendorf) 37; (Mark Gubin) 38
Frank Sloan: 25, 36

Edited by Marion Dane Bauer

Copyright © 1989 by Crestwood House, Macmillan Publishing Company

All rights reserved. No part of this book may be reproduced or transmitted in any form or by any means, electronic or mechanical, including photocopying, recording, or by any information storage and retrieval system, without permission in writing from the Publisher.

CRESTWOOD HOUSE

Macmillan Publishing Company
866 Third Avenue
New York, NY 10022
Collier Macmillan Canada, Inc.

Produced by Carnival Enterprises

Printed in the United States of America

First Edition

10 9 8 7 6 5 4 3 2 1

CONTENTS

Introducing New York City 5
    The Big Apple
    Overview of Things to Do
    What a Few Beads Bought
    The Five Boroughs
    Finding Your Way Around the Big Apple
    Transportation

Lower Manhattan: Downtown 12
    The Upper Bay and Lady Liberty
    Downtown and Wall Street
    Chinatown and City Hall
    Greenwich Village

Midtown Manhattan 29
    The Heart of the City
    The United Nations
    Rockefeller Center
    Three Floors of Toys
    Times Square

Uptown Manhattan 39
    Central Park
    Lincoln Center and Museums
    Harlem

You Will Want to Return 43
New York Statistics 44
For More Information 44
City Map 45
Index of People & Places 46

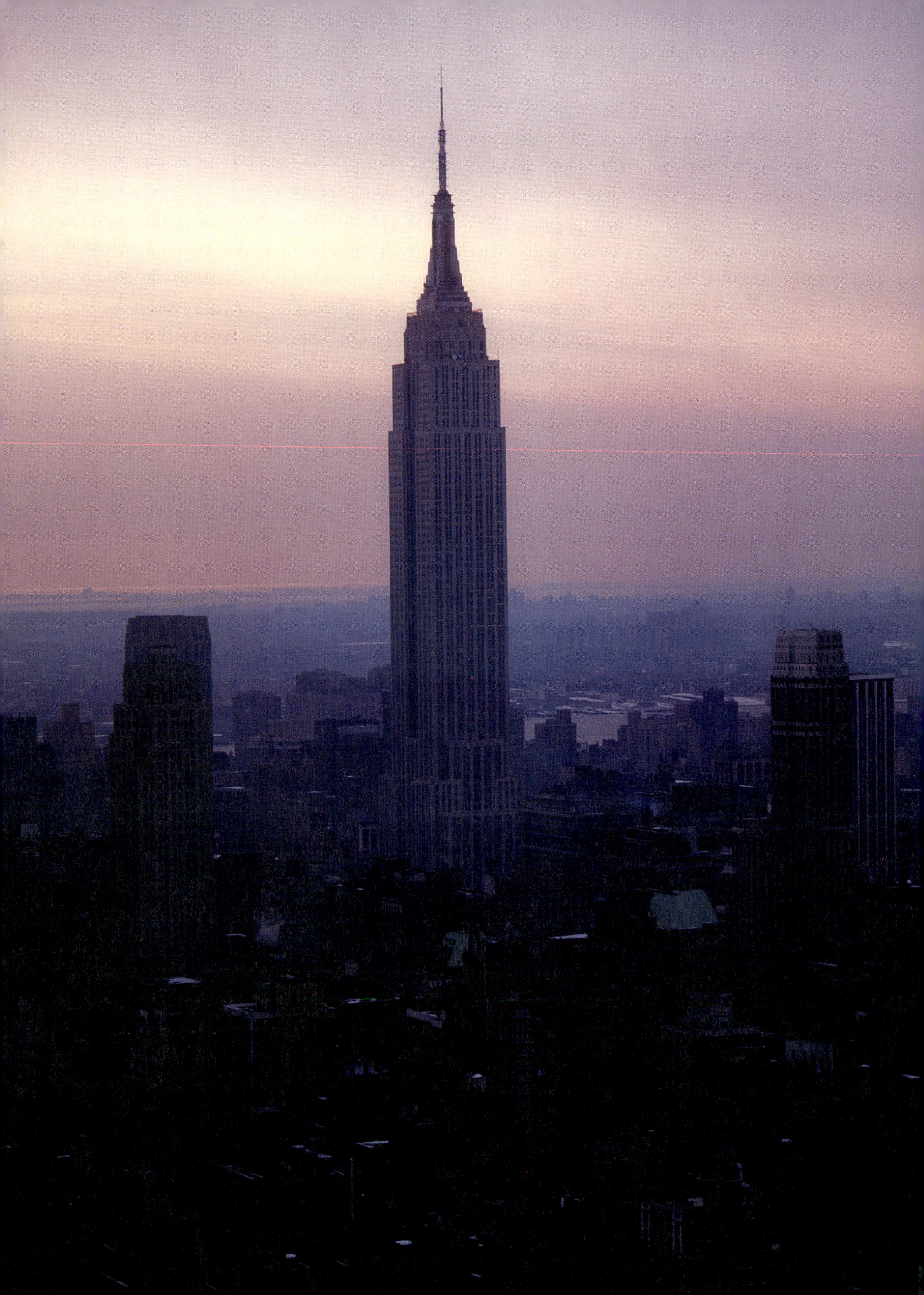

Introducing New York City

The Big Apple

There is an excitement about just the name "New York." This is the city called the "Big Apple." It is one of the best-known cities in the world.

New York is where the pace never slows and the day never ends. It is a pulsating, dynamic city. That is how the New York Convention and Visitors Bureau sees the city. The bureau also says it is a "city that changes its face almost daily."

There is a vitality in this city. The city's life doesn't halt with darkness, even though thousands of people leave **Manhattan** each workday afternoon. At night they return to their homes. Some live in one of New York City's other boroughs (counties). Others live on **Long Island**. Some have homes in Connecticut or New Jersey.

You might live in a small town or a good-sized city. No matter how many people live where you do, the number can't compare with the number of people who live in New York City. The city is the largest in the United States. About 7,263,000 people of all colors and creeds live here.

New York City is an island in the Atlantic Ocean, just off the far southeastern corner of New York state. Lying at the mouth of the **Hudson River**, it is one of the best natural harbors in the world.

Overview of Things to Do

Tourism is a big business in New York City. As a visitor, you will be one of many thousands of out-of-towners. The city has more than 17 million overnight visitors a year.

New York's biggest attractions include the world's most famous statue, the **Statue of Liberty**, and the **Empire State Building**, the most famous skyscraper in the world. The **United Nations**

The Empire State Building towers above Manhattan.

Headquarters, Central Park, and **Fifth Avenue** are also high on most tourists' lists.

What a Few Beads Bought

The bay that is now **New York Harbor** was first discovered by Europeans more than 350 years ago. Later, the Dutch established a permanent trading post on the southern tip of today's Manhattan Island. The post was built in 1626 by the Dutch East India Company, which was carrying on a successful trade with the Native Americans who lived here.

The man who made this trade possible was **Henry Hudson.** He was an English navigator and explorer who worked for Dutch business interests. He explored the river now named for him.

The island of Manhattan viewed from the air

The leader of that first Dutch settlement was **Peter Minuit**. He made what is now considered one of the best real estate deals in history. Minuit bought the whole island of Manhattan from the native residents. He paid them with glass beads, multicolored cloth, and steel knives. The value of these goods was about $24!

The Dutch called the settlement New Amsterdam. Twenty years later it had some 2,000 residents. Already there was a mixture of cultures. In 1664, New Amsterdam became New York when the Dutch surrendered it to English ships. Ten years later the Dutch recaptured the town. Briefly it became New Orange. The Prince of Orange was a member of Holland's ruling family.

The town was returned to England and again became New York in 1712. This took place as part of the settlement of a war between England and Holland. New York remained under the rule of British governors until the American Revolution. Then New York became the seat of the colonies' first national Congress. Later, the Continental Congress made it the country's first capital.

New York City remained the home of the new country's government after the adoption of the Constitution. **George Washington** was inaugurated here in 1789 as the first president of the United States.

The seat of the government was soon relocated. Philadelphia became the capital in 1790. In 1800, the nation's capital was moved to Washington, D.C., a city created for that purpose.

For some time, New York City remained the state capital. However, in 1800 the New York state government was moved upstate to **Albany**.

At this time, New York was a city of about 50,000 people. A century earlier it had been smaller than both Philadelphia and Boston. Even in 1800 the entire city of New York occupied only a few blocks. These were at the southern tip of Manhattan. People did live across the river in **Brooklyn**. But Brooklyn was then a separate city.

New York City's population grew with wave after wave of immigration. This began about the middle of the nineteenth century. There were some 20,000 New York City residents in 1776. By 1850 there were about 500,000 New Yorkers.

The opening of the **Erie Canal** was important to the city's growth. This took place in 1825. The canal linked the Hudson River with Lake Erie. This established a water route to the West through the Great Lakes. The canal proved to be a tremendous boost to New York's economy.

New York City became America's major commercial and financial center. The canal was a prime factor. So was the founding of the Bank of New York by **Alexander Hamilton**, who was also one of the nation's founders.

The city prospered and grew. By 1880, its population was more than 1,200,000. Major immigration from Europe continued after World War I and II. Now new residents come to New York from Southeast Asia and the Soviet Union. They make the city a diverse and fascinating place.

The Five Boroughs

Today, almost one and one-half million people live in Manhattan.

Each workday, millions more come here to work in huge high-rise buildings. These structures provide the dramatic skyline familiar to visitors.

Despite its huge population, New York City does not occupy much space. The island of Manhattan is a relatively small place in terms of the land it covers. It is 2.3 miles wide at its widest point. It is only 0.8 mile wide at its narrowest point. It is just under 13.5 miles long. All of Manhattan occupies only 22 square miles.

Manhattan is the place most people mean when they say New York City. This book is about Manhattan.

New York City actually consists of five counties, also called boroughs. In addition to Manhattan, they are the **Bronx**, Brooklyn, **Queens**, and **Staten Island**. The boroughs were unified under the Greater New York Charter in 1887. It became effective the first day of the following year.

Of the five boroughs, only the Bronx is on the mainland. Staten Island and Manhattan are both islands. Queens and Brooklyn are both on the western end of Long Island.

The Brooklyn Bridge connects Brooklyn and Manhattan.

Manhattan is separated from the Bronx by the **Harlem River**. The Hudson River flows south down the west sides of the Bronx and Manhattan and separates New York from the state of New Jersey. The **East River** (which is actually a strait) flows along the east sides of the Bronx and Manhattan.

The five boroughs and New Jersey are linked by tunnels, bridges, and ferries. To see all five boroughs you can take a bus tour or a cruise. Grayline Tours offers many guided bus trips. The Circle Line's three-hour sightseeing cruise goes around the island of Manhattan. These tours are relaxing, but somewhat expensive, ways to see much of the entire city.

If you have a large budget, there is another option. You can take a sightseeing helicopter trip. The helicopters fly from one of the several heliports in Manhattan.

Finding Your Way Around the Big Apple

It is quite easy to find your way around Manhattan. The entire midtown and upper Manhattan sections are laid out in a gridiron pattern of streets and avenues. All numbered streets run east and west (crosstown). All avenues run south (downtown) and north (uptown).

The problem is choosing what to do in Manhattan. There are so many possibilities.

A good place to begin is the New York Convention and Visitors Bureau. It is located at the southwest corner of Central Park at 59th Street. Here you can pick up helpful tips plus maps and mass-transit information. The bureau also has free individual folders on the other four boroughs.

Transportation

Most people avoid driving on congested Manhattan streets. Parking spaces are not always available, either. But there are almost 12,000 taxis in New York.

There is also New York City's public transportation system. It is "unmatched in any other city," according to the New York Convention and Visitors Bureau. They also say it is "vast, efficient, safe, and inexpensive."

There are 230 miles of subway lines and 1,745 miles of bus routes in the city. The subways and buses are used by over 5 million riders each weekday.

New to New York City's transportation scene is the exciting aerial tramway. The tramway, on 2nd Avenue at East 60th Street, takes you to the "new city" on **Roosevelt Island**. This is the long, narrow island in the East River between upper Manhattan and Queens.

Once you get to the section of the city you want to tour, walking is one of the best ways to see it.

New York's aerial tramway takes visitors from Manhattan to Roosevelt Island.

The New York skyline, capped by the two square towers of the World Trade Center. The South Street Seaport is in the foreground.

Lower Manhattan: Downtown

One way to see Manhattan is to work from bottom to top. Begin at the southern end of the island and work your way north. You can spend many days covering these few miles.

The southern tip of the island is lower Manhattan. It is also called downtown. This area is less than a quarter of a square mile. Within this small space is a major waterfront, one of the world's most important shipping and trade districts, and the world's most famous financial area, **Wall Street**.

Lower Manhattan runs from the tip of the island to **City Hall Park**. This park surrounds **City Hall** at Broadway and Murray Street. Lower Manhattan is the oldest section of the city. Its narrow streets turn and twist. They were built by the first Dutch settlers.

Today, skyscraper after skyscraper blot out the sun. Early on, it became obvious that for Manhattan to house the number of people who wanted to work or live there, the only way to build was up. One of the first skyscrapers, the 20-story **Flatiron Building,** was built in 1903. Now skyscrapers dominate the island.

At the far southern tip of Manhattan is a small park known as **Battery Park**. It is between State Street and the Hudson River seawall. It takes its name from a post established there in 1693. The British called the park Oyster Pasty Battery.

The decorative Flatiron Building was one of the earliest skyscrapers in New York City.

Monuments that you can visit in Battery Park include a reconstructed fort, called **Castle Clinton National Monument**. The original fort was built in 1807. Castle Clinton was named a national monument in 1950. Exhibits show how it was used over the years. It is open daily except Christmas Day.

The Upper Bay and Lady Liberty

While in Battery Park, go to its seawall. Look south over the Upper Bay section of the New York Harbor. The Hudson River enters the harbor on the west, the East River on the east. Across the Hudson River you can see New Jersey.

Southwest from the park are the Statue of Liberty and **Ellis Island**. Only 500 yards away you can see **Governors Island**.

The Statue of Liberty is in New York Harbor, southwest of Manhattan.

A military base still exists on Governors Island, in the foreground.

This 173-acre-island is where the colonial governors lived. Today it is the United States Coast Guard's largest base. Governors Island is known for its tight security. It is open to the public only two days a year.

"Lady Liberty" is something almost every visitor wants to see. The statue is located on **Liberty Island** in New York Harbor. It is a mile and a half southwest of Manhattan. It is just off the New Jersey coast.

Castle Clinton serves as the boat dock for boarding the ferry to the Statue of Liberty. Circle Line ferries leave Battery Park seven days a week for the ten-minute ride to Liberty Island.

Lady Liberty has lifted her lamp since 1886. Her multimillion-dollar restoration was finished in 1986, in time for the statue's centennial celebration.

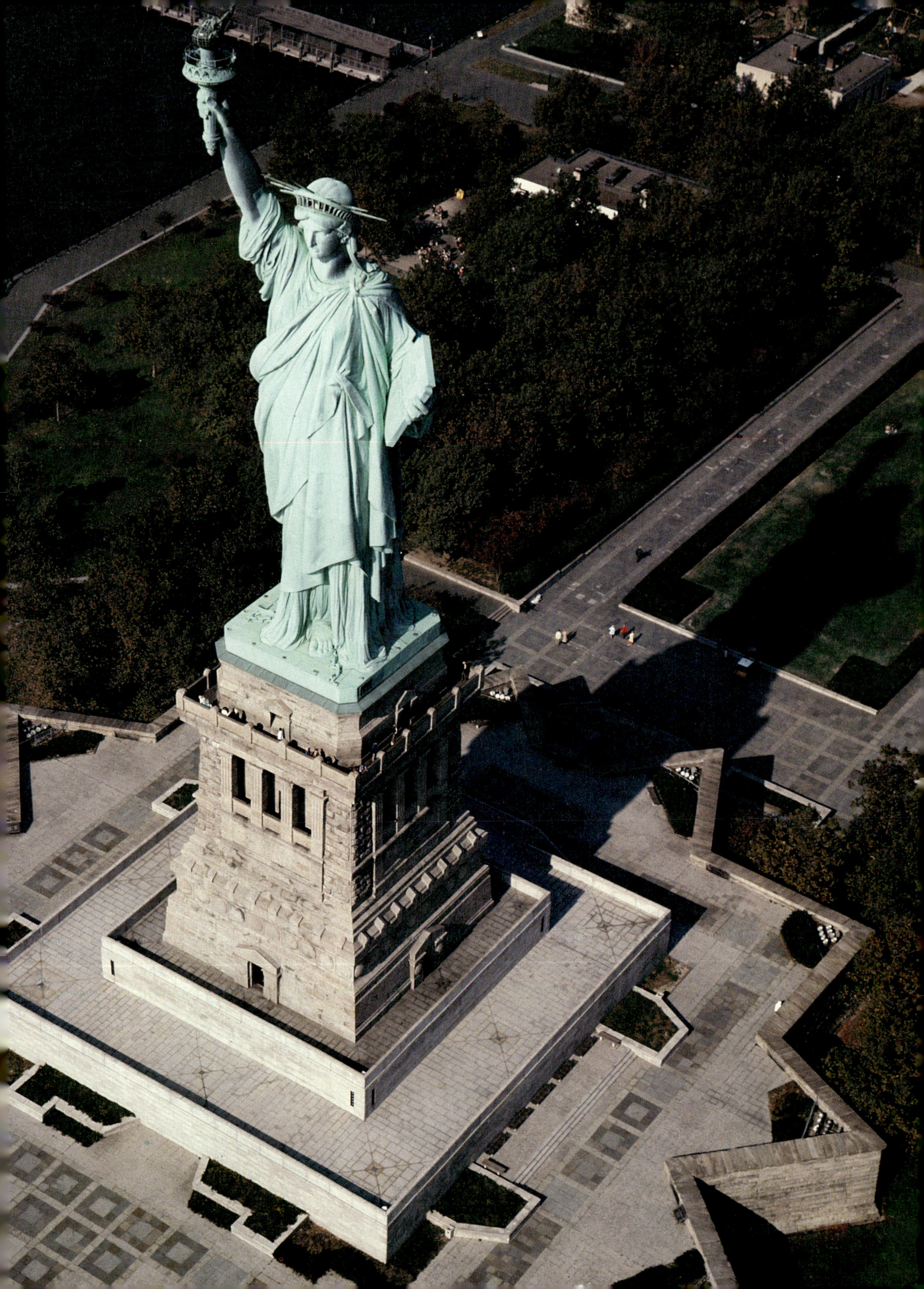

The huge statue is a national monument. It portrays liberty as a woman stepping free of broken shackles. She extends a flaming torch in her right hand. In her left hand she carries a tablet. The tablet represents the Declaration of Independence.

The statue is 151 feet tall and stands on a pedestal. The tip of the torch is 305 feet above ground level. Lady Liberty is the work of French sculptor **Frédéric-Auguste Bartholdi**.

Bartholdi spent ten years working on the project. Copper sheeting was shaped over carved wooden forms. This was done by hammering the sheets by hand. Bartholdi built the statue in France, section by section. It was shipped to New York where it was put together on the island.

The statue was a gift from the people of France to the people of the United States. The original statue cost over $250,000. The money was provided by contributions from residents in more than 180 French communities. The statue and its pedestal were paid for in part by donations from Americans. Many schoolchildren made contributions.

Over the years, the statue's copper exterior suffered from exposure to the weather. Many other repairs were needed. This brought about the massive restoration job.

Your visit to the statue includes an elevator ride that stops at a balcony. This runs around the top of the statue's pedestal. Here you can look out in all directions. It's a great view on a clear day. There are descriptions telling what you are looking at.

If you want a view from an even higher spot, you can climb 168 steps to reach the observation platform at Lady Liberty's crown. It offers a wonderful view of the harbor, Ellis Island, and both the Manhattan and Brooklyn skylines.

You also will want to visit the **American Museum of Immigration**. This is in the base of the Statue of Liberty. There are exhibits telling the story of immigration to the United States. These relate how the statue came to be the symbol of the United States.

In this museum, as well as on the statue's pedestal, is the famous poem about Lady Liberty. Written by **Emma Lazarus**, it

An elevator takes visitors to the balcony on the Statue of Liberty's pedestal. From there, visitors can climb the 168 steps to the top of the statue.

includes the well-known lines: "Give me your tired, your poor, your huddled masses yearning to breathe free."

Just north of Liberty Island is Ellis Island. From 1890 to 1943, Ellis Island was the primary immigration center in the United States. Millions passed through here. The ships on which they arrived first went by the welcoming arms of Lady Liberty. At the peak of immigration, more than one million newcomers were processed here in a year. The immigration center was moved to Manhattan when Ellis Island was closed.

Ellis Island became part of the Statue of Liberty National Monument in 1965. It was opened to tourists eleven years later by the National Park Service.

The Staten Island Ferry takes New Yorkers from Manhattan to Staten Island and back.

A turn-of-the-century firehouse juts into the harbor off Battery Park.

While in Lower Manhattan, you might want to take the ferry to Staten Island. The ride offers a great view of New York Harbor and the Lower Manhattan skyline. The ferry passes by Governors, Liberty, and Ellis islands as well. The **Staten Island Ferry** terminal is located on the east side of Battery Park.

Downtown and Wall Street

After you travel across New York Harbor, you can put your walking shoes back on. There is still much to see in Lower Manhattan.

When this area was still New Amsterdam, the first road was built sometime around 1700. It linked the settlement with a sub-

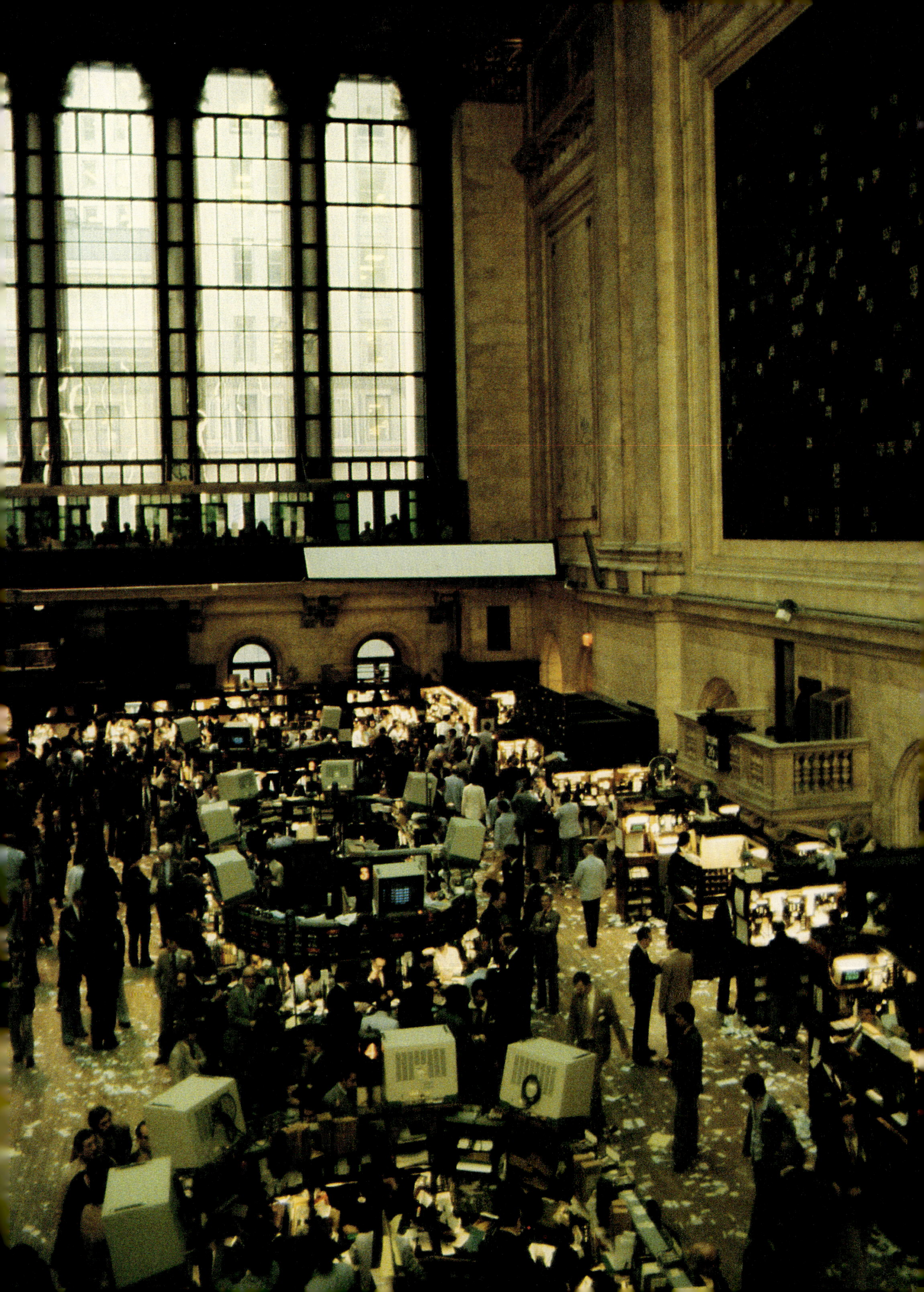

urban village called New Harlem. That road was called **Broadway**. Today Broadway is one of the world's most famous streets. It begins at Battery Park and runs north throughout Manhattan into the Bronx.

Begin your walking trip on Broadway. Start at **Bowling Green**, a tiny park at the foot of Broadway near Battery Park. Bowling Green bounds Battery Park on the north. It is supposed to be the place where the purchase of Manhattan Island took place.

A short walk north takes you to Wall Street, halfway between the Battery and City Hall. This short street has been the center of downtown Manhattan's financial district since 1792. In that year brokers met under a tree at that location to draw up an agreement. They agreed to form what later became the **New York Stock Exchange**.

Today Wall Street's buildings include the New York Stock Exchange, the **Federal Reserve Bank**, and a variety of other financial institutions. There are also government offices on Wall Street.

Put a tour of the New York Stock Exchange on your schedule. The Exchange is located at Wall and Broad streets. This is your chance to see the money capital of the world. Some consider the Exchange one of the city's best sightseeing bargains.

There are free tours during weekday trading hours. Visitors can look down upon the Exchange floor from a second-floor gallery. The activity at the Exchange is described by a narration.

Nearby is the **American Stock Exchange**. This is the nation's other major stock exchange.

The **Federal Hall National Memorial** is at the corner of Wall and Nassau streets. It occupies a building put up in 1842 on the site of Federal Hall. That is where George Washington took his oath of office. Inside the memorial are mementos from Revolutionary history.

Downtown you can see the city's tallest building and the second-tallest building in the United States—**The World Trade Center.** Its 1,377 feet are topped only by The Sears Tower in Chicago, which is 104 feet taller. The center's twin towers are each 110 stories tall. They seem to stand as guards over New York City's harbor.

The New York Stock Exchange bustles with activity.

A view of the twin towers of the World Trade Center, from a marina in New Jersey

Visitors can enjoy some great views of the city from the top of the World Trade Center. One viewing spot is a glass-enclosed gallery. This is on the 107th floor at 2 World Trade Center (the South Tower). The rooftop observation deck on the 110th floor is the world's highest open-air deck. On a clear day you can see farther than 50 miles. The view from the deck is particularly stunning at sunset. The gallery and deck are open daily. There is an admission charge.

For an unusual experience, watch commodities traders in action. You can do this at the **Commodities Exchange Center**. It is at 4 World Trade Center. There is a ninth-floor visitors' gallery. From here you can watch the commotion on the floor during trading hours.

Visitors can eat seafood and enjoy walking around a paddleboat and sailing ships at the South Street Seaport.

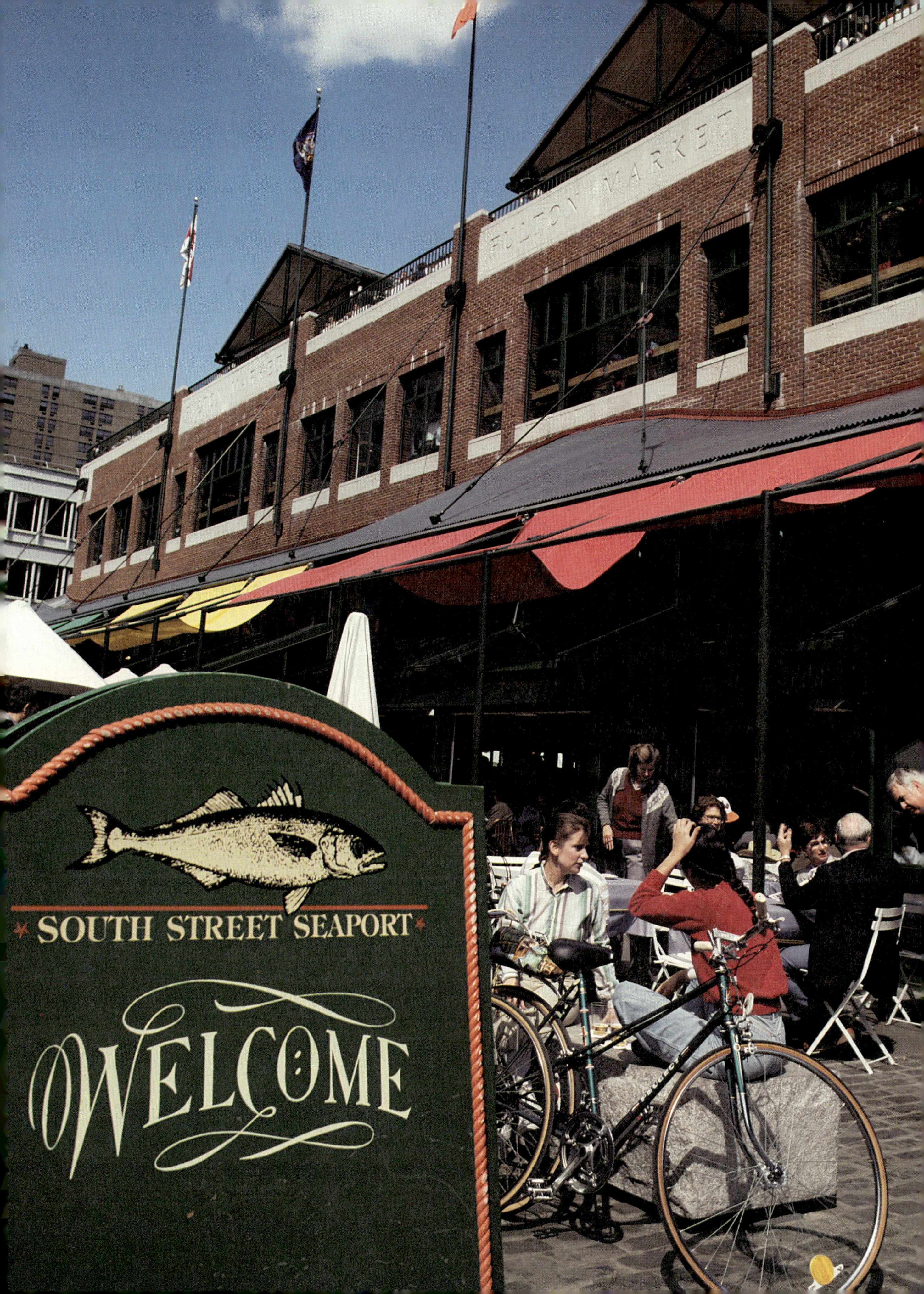
FULTON MARKET
SOUTH STREET SEAPORT
WELCOME

East of the World Trade Center is a fascinating area. Walk on Fulton Street to the **South Street Seaport**. It is along the East River waterfront. This is an indoor-outdoor "museum" made up of eleven blocks and three piers. The piers stretch along the river.

The entire area has been restored to the way it looked in the nineteenth century when it was one of the world's great ports for sailing ships.

Today, visitors can see five square-rigged sailing ships docked near a side-wheel paddleboat. They are from around the turn of the century. The ships are docked at Pier 16. Pier 17 offers outstanding views of the river, as well as stores and restaurants.

Another sight to see at the Seaport is an old printing shop. A model-ship museum and the **Titanic Memorial Lighthouse** are also worth visiting. The South Street Seaport Museum offers tours and visits to ships.

Shoppers and the chefs of big restaurants look for the best seafood bargains at the Fulton Fish Market.

New York's City Hall, where the mayor's office is located

Also located at the Seaport is the famous **Fulton Fish Market**—once the largest wholesale fish market on the Atlantic Coast.

Chinatown and City Hall

Continue your tour of Manhattan by going to City Hall Park. This park bridges downtown and the **Lower East Side**. In July 1776, George Washington was among a crowd who gathered in the park to hear a reading of the Declaration of Independence.

In the park is City Hall. It was built between 1803 and 1811. It is considered to be one of the most attractive public buildings in the country. It was renovated in 1956.

The approach to the **Brooklyn Bridge** begins on the east side of City Hall Park. You can take a walk across the bridge to Brook-

The Brooklyn Bridge is one of the best-known suspension bridges in the country.

lyn. Even walking partway across the bridge will give you a good view of Lower Manhattan. The Brooklyn Bridge was an engineering marvel when it opened in 1883. It still ranks among the great suspension bridges in the world.

Chinatown is just west of Chatham Square. You enter Chinatown from the south just off Worth Street. You will want to take in Chinatown's own sights and sounds. Here, even the telephone booths are different. They look like small pagodas (two towers with roofs that curve upward).

Today, Chinatown is the home of thousands of Chinese. They live in a very small area of twisting streets. This area has been the home of the city's large Chinese community for over 100 years. By 1876, some 200 Chinese had established homes and businesses on Mott Street.

Just north of Chinatown is **Canal Street**, one of Manhattan's busiest crosstown streets. It carries traffic between New Jersey and Brooklyn from the Holland Tunnel to the Manhattan Bridge. The Holland was the first of the tunnels built under the Hudson River. The Manhattan Bridge crosses to Brooklyn, and traffic can go on to Long Island.

From Canal Street turn onto Mulberry Street and you'll feel as though you have entered Italy. **Little Italy** is a quiet Italian neighborhood filled with a variety of restaurants. Every year the Feast of San Gennaro, the patron saint of Naples, is held in September.

East of Little Italy is the area known as the Lower East Side. The Lower East Side was once the melting pot of the city. This was during and after the large-scale immigration to New York City. This immigration began in the latter part of the nineteenth century. People of many different nationalities moved into this neighborhood.

Thousands of Chinese-Americans live and work in the area known as Chinatown.

Walk a half block north of Canal Street if you want to participate in the experience of light. The **Museum of Holography** offers you this chance.

You may have studied holograms in school. They are three-dimensional images. They are formed by the interaction of laser light waves on a piece of (usually) coated glass or film. Light seems to come from within the art displayed in the museum.

Greenwich Village

One of Manhattan's best-known areas is **Greenwich Village** (pronounced Gren-ich) on the Lower West Side of Manhattan. Greenwich Village actually isn't a village at all. It is an area between the Hudson River waterfront and Broadway. It is between 14th Street on the north and Spring Street on the south.

The Greenwich Village area was a Native American village when the first Dutch settlers came. It later became the site of country estates and mansions owned by the wealthy and famous. Many of these beautiful buildings are still standing today. The village also harbors many wonderful antique shops, book and record stores, and boutiques. At night, it comes alive with clubs where you can hear rock, jazz, or blues, and see all kinds of people on parade in the streets.

At the center of Greenwich Village is **Washington Square**. Look for the Washington Arch in the square. The arch was built in 1895 as a memorial to the nation's first president. Washington Square was the last part of the village to be developed. It had been the city's potter's field, a burial place for the friendless poor.

New York University, one of the city's major universities, is here. The campus runs along the east side of Washington Square. Fifth Avenue begins its journey northward from the Washington Arch.

If you like fire engines, head south to Spring Street to the **New York City Fire Museum**. On display are items showing the history of firefighting in New York City.

An aerial view of Washington Square, in the center of Greenwich Village

Midtown Manhattan

The Heart of the City

The heart of the city—midtown Manhattan—is a small area. It runs south from Central Park for less than a mile and a half. The distance between the East and Hudson rivers in this area is a mile and three quarters. But it would take weeks, not days, to see everything of interest here.

Large ocean-going ships dock along the piers on the Hudson River. So does the tremendous aircraft carrier the **U.S.S. Intrepid**, which is open to the public.

Across the island on the East River is the United Nations. In between the rivers is the Empire State Building, **Times Square**, and the Broadway theater district. The wondrous **Rockefeller Center** is also here. So is the famous Fifth Avenue shopping area.

Begin your tour of midtown after visiting the piers on the Hudson. Just south of the piers is the mammoth **Jacob K. Javits Convention Center**. It overlooks the Hudson River. It is the largest such center in the world. It occupies 22 acres over five blocks.

One of the country's most famous sports arenas is **Madison Square Garden**. It is the home of pro basketball's New York Knickerbockers and pro hockey's New York Rangers. It is also the site of rock concerts and championship boxing and tennis.

The Garden is built above **Pennsylvania Station**. This is the

The skating rink at Rockefeller Center

At dusk, New York's skyline lights up with color.

world's busiest railroad station. A 29-story office building also towers above Penn Station.

Walk two blocks east and you are in the center of Manhattan at the Empire State Building. This was once the world's tallest building. It is 1,250 feet high plus its 164-foot television transmitting mast. Now more than 50 years old, it remains as popular as ever with visitors.

The upper floors of this skyscraper are lit up at night. The colors of the lights are changed each season. The 102-story building was finished in 1931. The main shaft of the building rises from a broad five-story base.

Go to the observation decks on the 86th and 102nd floors of the Empire State Building. Here you can enjoy breathtaking views

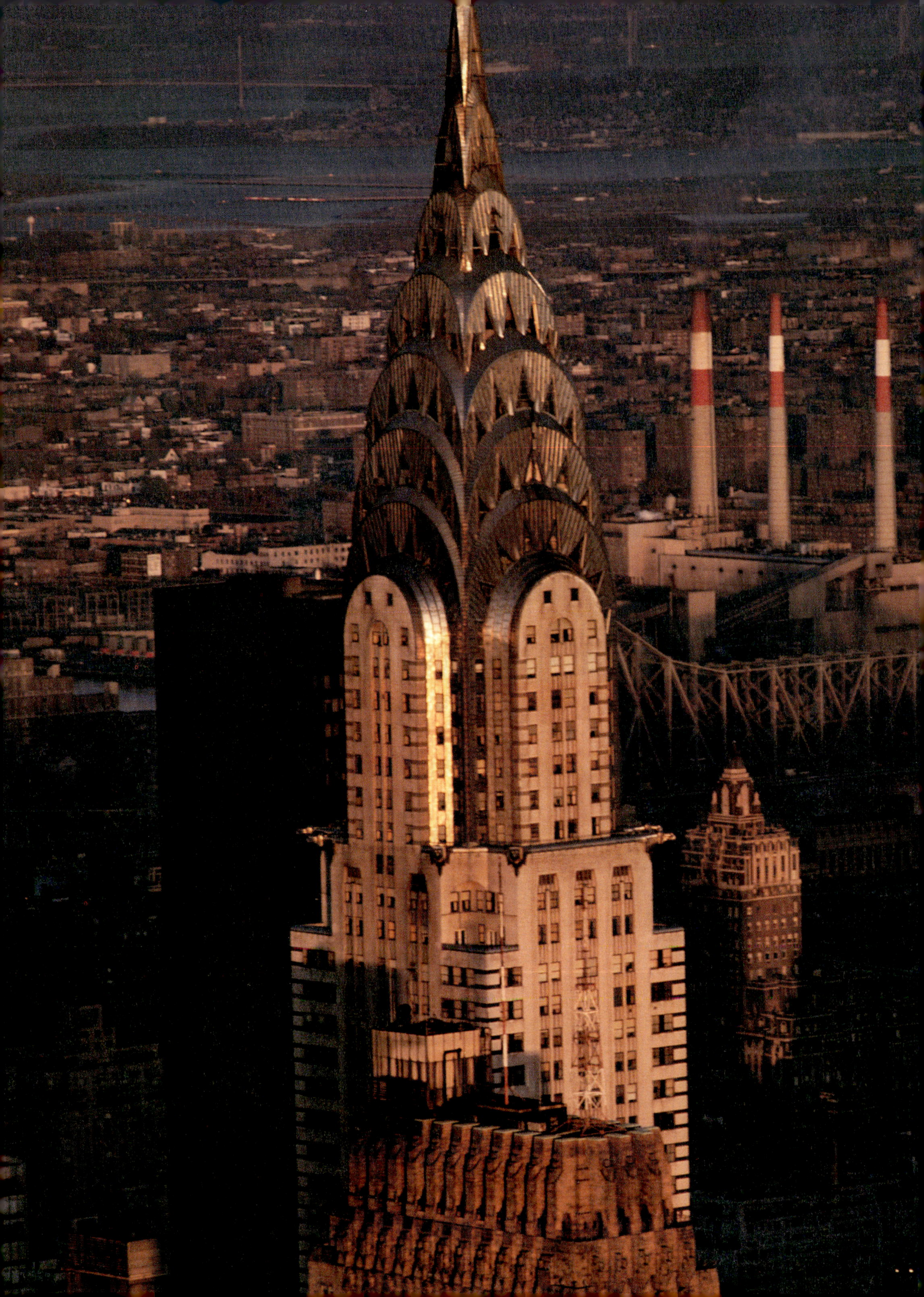

of the city and beyond. If you get a clear day, you can see over 50 miles.

The **Guinness World Records Exhibit Hall** is also open daily. It is on the concourse level of the Empire State Building. Here there are exhibits dealing with the records cited in the well-known book.

Next, head north on Fifth Avenue to 42nd Street. On East 42nd at Park Avenue is **Grand Central Terminal**. This is an engineering masterpiece. It also is famous for its architectural style. Inside are two levels of tracks. More than 550 trains travel over these tracks each day. The station's main concourse is one of the largest rooms in the world. There are free tours once a week.

Across the street is a branch of the famed **Whitney Museum of American Art**.

A block farther east is the **Chrysler Building**. It was the tallest in the world when it was built in 1930. The Empire State Building surpassed it a year later. The Chrysler Building's unusual spire is a great example of art deco architecture. Look for it at night when it is lit up.

The United Nations

You will want to make some time for a visit to the United Nations. Here the world comes to New York.

The United Nations was founded shortly after World War II. Fifty nations signed the United Nations charter. They did this in San Francisco in 1945. The United Nations moved into its Manhattan quarters in 1952. Now more than 150 nations are members. The membership ranges from Afghanistan to Zimbabwe and includes the United States and other major nations.

The members of the United Nations discuss problems among nations. Its founders hoped it could be a major force for peace in the world. The United Nations has solved disputes between nations and has helped to halt armed conflicts.

Most of the United Nations's work takes place on 18 acres overlooking the East River.

The visitors' entrance to the United Nations Headquarters, a

The Chrysler Building's spire rises above midtown Manhattan.

The Security Council chamber at the United Nations

marble and limestone building, is at the north end of the General Assembly Building.

Try to attend a session at the United Nations. Visitors are welcome at most of them. A limited number of tickets are issued to attend official meetings. There is no charge. However, there are no advance schedules of meetings. So sometimes there are last-minute changes. Therefore, most tickets to visitors are issued only a few minutes before meetings are to begin. And they are issued on a first-come, first-served basis. You can get tickets for meetings in the lobby of the headquarters building.

Delegates from the member nations, of course, speak many languages. It is interesting how the United Nations deals with this fact. It has five official languages. They are Chinese, English,

French, Russian, and Spanish. At most meetings there are interpreters. They interpret speeches in each of the five languages.

When you attend a meeting, you will see earphones at the visitors' seats. Use them to listen to what is being said. You can dial into the language you want to hear.

There are tours of the headquarters building each day.

Other major buildings in the United Nations complex include the Conference and the Secretariat buildings. There is also the **Hammarskjöld Library** off 42nd Street.

From the gardens on the United Nations grounds, you can look out over the East River. The long island that extends to the north is Roosevelt Island. It was once a prison. Now the island is home to hospitals and housing units.

Rockefeller Center

The United Nations belongs to the world. Rockefeller Center belongs to New York City. It is west of the United Nations, toward the center of midtown Manhattan.

This Manhattan landmark was 50 years old in 1982. It has been called "a city within a city." It is the largest privately owned business and entertainment complex in the world. Its 19 buildings are all connected by underground concourses.

You can ice skate in the center's sunken plaza. This is one of the best known parts of the center. The plaza is often photographed in movies. It is used for dining in the summer.

The center is also the home of the famous **Radio City Music Hall Entertainment Center**. Much of the entertainment offered is family oriented. You are in for a special treat if you can buy tickets for the annual *Magnificent Christmas Spectacular*. This is presented by Radio City Music Hall for about eight weeks beginning in mid-November. Almost a quarter-million people see this show each year.

Radio City Music Hall is known for its dancers, the Rockettes. Backstage tours of the music hall are available Monday through Saturday.

Visitors to New York can take a backstage tour of the famous Radio City Music Hall.

Have you ever wondered how a television show is produced? Take a guided tour of a television or radio studio at the **National Broadcasting Company** (NBC) at Rockefeller Center. You can also watch a game show or soap opera being taped, if you write for tickets in advance.

Rockefeller Center is a fun place to wander around as well. There are hundreds and hundreds of stores, shops, and restaurants. The gardens of Rockefeller Center draw millions of visitors each year.

A famous church, **Saint Patrick's Cathedral**, is across from Rockefeller Plaza. Its towers are 330 feet high. Work on the church began in 1858, but wasn't completed until 1906.

Three Floors of Toys

New York's famous retail shopping area runs between 34th and 59th streets on Fifth Avenue. Here are such well-known stores as **Saks Fifth Avenue** and **Bergdorf Goodman**.

For kids, a must stop is **F.A.O. Schwartz**, the famous toy store. Its goods capture the imagination of both children and adults. There are three floors of toys to see.

Fashionable apartment buildings line Park Avenue.

After checking out the toys you can meet an eight-foot robot. Gordon is a see-through humanoid robot that can talk. Gordon is found in the **AT&T Infoquest Center** on the fourth floor of AT&T's Manhattan corporate headquarters.

Here high tech is low key. A free, entertaining tour shows visitors the world of computers, software, and fiber optics (light-wave communications). There are hands-on learning opportunities, too.

A stop at the Museum of Modern Art (also known as "MOMA") will complete your tour of Midtown. It houses some of the most famous photographs and paintings of the nineteenth and twentieth centuries by such artists as Vincent Van Gogh, Pablo Picasso, and Alfred Steiglitz. It has some of the most striking furniture as well, including a chair in the shape of a baseball mitt.

The billboard lights at Times Square have earned it the nickname "The Great White Way."

Times Square

You can't visit Manhattan without seeing the excitement and glitter of Times Square. You also will want to see the bright lights of Broadway. So head west of Rockefeller Plaza to Broadway.

South on Broadway is the theater district. Such productions as *Cats, West Side Story,* and *A Chorus Line* have opened on this famous strip. For many years, young men and women have come here from across the country and throughout the world. They have dreamed of becoming stars in plays or musicals. A few have made it.

Times Square stretches from 47th to 42nd streets at the intersection of Broadway and Seventh Avenue. At night, huge lit-up signs give a particular brilliance to the area. These signs have given Times Square the name "The Great White Way." Thousands of people come to Times Square each December 31. They come to celebrate the coming of the new year at midnight. For one night, they make Times Square America's town square.

Uptown Manhattan

Central Park

Central Park dominates the northern part of Manhattan. This famous park runs from West 59th Street to West 110th Street. The park is between Fifth Avenue and Central Park West. The park's entire 840 acres are surrounded by a masonry wall. The wall is broken by numerous entrances.

Central Park is a great place for people watching. You'll see joggers, bicycle riders, and strollers. They use the park's paths and roads. On summer weekends there are street performers and free concerts.

There are many beautifully landscaped areas in the park, as well as several recreational areas. There also are lakes, ponds, wooded areas, fountains, and statues. One of the ponds is used for model sailboats in nice weather.

Joggers, hikers, bicyclists, even horseback riders, enjoy Central Park.

A children's zoo, designed for young boys and girls, is located south of 65th Street. There is also an ice skating rink, a carousel, and two rowing lakes. A castle, **The Belvedere,** is at West 79th Street. Stories are told at the Hans Christian Andersen statue on Saturday mornings, when the weather is warm.

Lincoln Center and Museums

On either side of the park are some of the nation's best-known museums and cultural centers. Just west of the park is **Lincoln Center for the Performing Arts**.

The center is the home of symphony and chamber orchestras, theater, the Metropolitan Opera, and ballet. The well-known **Juilliard School of Music** is here, too. That is where some of the most talented young musicians in the country go to school. Guided tours of the entire center are held each day.

The **American Museum of Natural History** is several blocks north. This museum is famous the world over. It has an extraordinary exhibit of real dinosaur skeletons and fossils. Its Halls of Peoples present life-size dioramas that show how people live from China to Peru. The museum is open daily.

Next door is the **Hayden Planetarium**. The building's dome serves as a screen. On it the movement of the stars and planets are realistically reproduced. There are laser rock shows on the weekends.

Across Central Park is one of the world's leading art museums. The **Metropolitan Museum of Art** is at 82nd Street and Fifth Avenue. It is the largest art museum in the western hemisphere. In addition to some of the world's greatest paintings, it has a Chinese garden and the swords and armor of medieval knights.

A few blocks south of the Metropolitan Museum is the Whitney Museum of American Art. It has the largest collection of paintings, sculptures, and drawings by twentieth-century artists at any public institution. It also shows movies and displays photographs of artists working today.

Farther north is the **Guggenheim Museum**. Its specialties are modern painting, sculpture, and graphic arts. Shaped like a corkscrew, the building itself is a work of art.

Harlem

Manhattan extends north of Central Park for about another 80 blocks. At its northern end, it is only a few blocks wide. In between there and Central Park is **Harlem**. Most of Harlem lies north of Central Park. Its boundaries are roughly 96th Street on the south and 178th Street on the north. Amsterdam and Lexington avenues might be considered its eastern and western boundaries.

Harlem first was settled by the Dutch in the seventeenth century. They called the area New Harlem. It remained rural farmland for 200 years. People began to move there when the Harlem Railroad was built in the 1830s.

Like the Lower East Side, Harlem has been a melting pot. It was a fashionable neighborhood in the late 1800s. Germans were the dominant nationality. There were also many Irish. Jews and Italians came to Harlem in the immigration waves of the 1880s and 1890s.

Blacks, or African-Americans, from lower Manhattan began moving to Harlem in 1910. Blacks from the south and the West Indies came during World War I. Harlem came to be associated throughout the world with black culture. People come from miles around to hear black musicians, see black dancers, and attend important lectures and sermons. The most recent newcomers to

Graduates and their families gather for the graduation ceremony at Columbia University.

Harlem have been from Puerto Rico and other Latin American countries.

One way to see Harlem is to take a sightseeing bus tour. Several companies offer these tours.

Just southwest of Harlem is the nation's sixth oldest university. **Columbia University** is also one of the country's most respected schools. It was chartered in 1754 as King's College. Columbia is just north of Central Park in an area known as Morningside Heights.

North of Harlem, Manhattan grows very narrow. Here, high above the Hudson River, is **Fort Tryon Park**. This is a wooded area that offers a great vantage point for overlooking the Hudson. From here you can also see the George Washington Bridge crossing the Hudson to New Jersey.

In Fort Tryon Park is **The Cloisters**. This is a branch of the Metropolitan Museum of Art. This unusual building is a museum of medieval jewels, tapestries, statues, and paintings. It includes parts of medieval monasteries and chapels brought from Europe. They were rebuilt stone by stone.

You Will Want to Return

Two things will probably be true about your visit to New York City. One will be that you didn't have enough time to see everything you wanted to see. The second will be that you will want to come back.

You will be drawn back by your desire to absorb all that Manhattan has to offer—the history, the parks, the shopping, the museums, music, plays, and sporting events.

You will also be drawn back by your desire to see again the towering buildings, to walk the famous streets, and to mingle with the crowds and watch the people.

New York Statistics

Population (as of the 1986 census): 7,262,700
Most populated borough: Brooklyn (2,293,200 people)
Least populated borough: Staten Island (374,000 people)
Miles of streets in New York: 6,400
Miles of waterfront: 578
Miles of beaches: 14.3
Number of parks and playgrounds: 1,543
Number of churches: 3,500
Number of first-class hotel rooms: 100,000
Number of restaurants: 25,000
Number of museums: 150
Theater: During the 1987-88 season, over 8 million theatergoers saw plays in 38 Broadway theaters.

For More Information

For more information about New York, write to:

New York Convention & Visitors
  Bureau, Inc.
2 Columbus Circle
New York, NY 10019

City Map

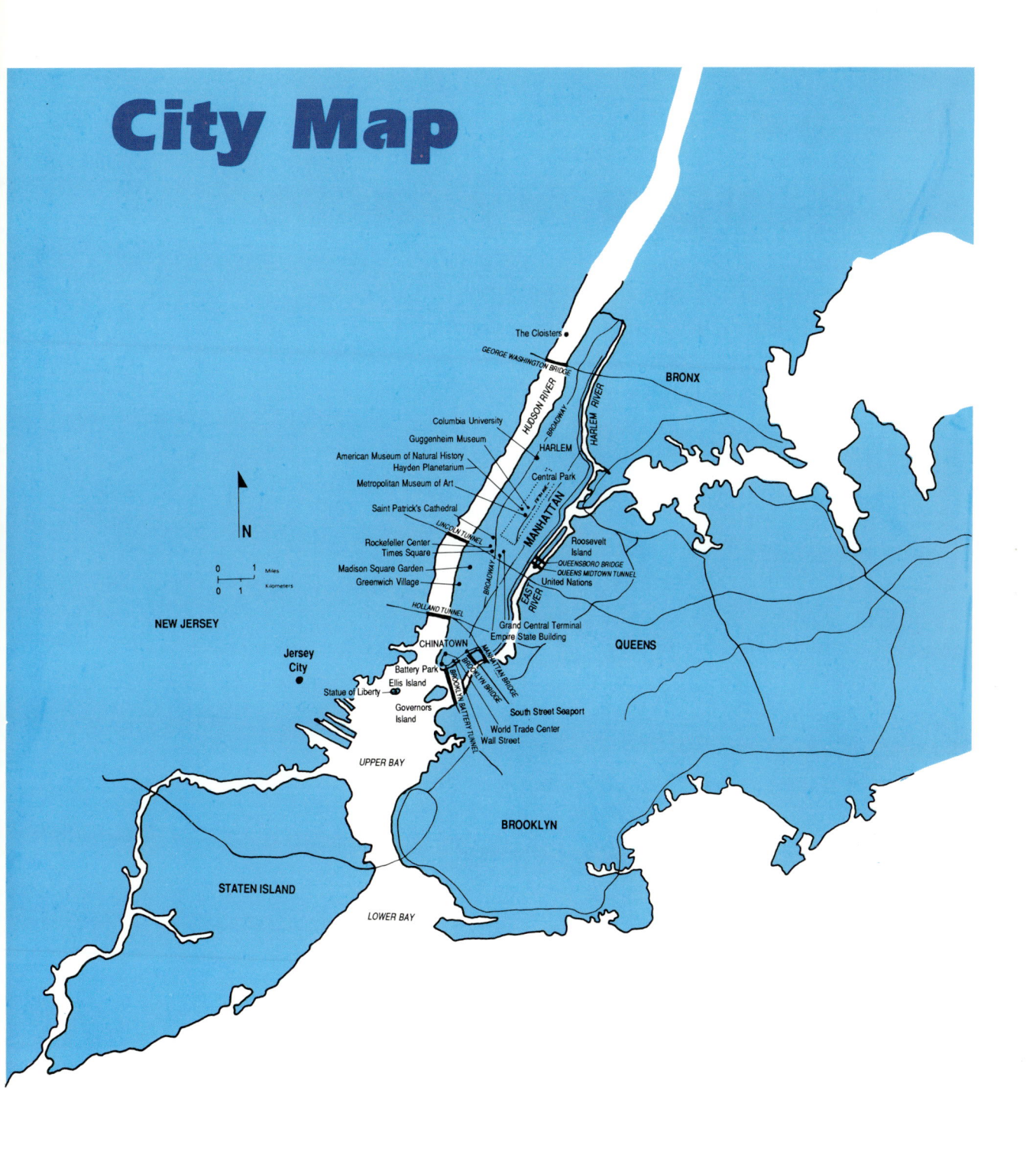

New York, New York

Index of People & Places

Albany, New York *7*
American Museum of Immigration *17*
American Museum of Natural History *41*
American Stock Exchange *21*
AT&T Infoquest Center *38*
Bartholdi, Frédéric-Auguste *17*
Battery Park *13, 14, 15, 19, 21*
Belvedere, The *40*
Bergdorf Goodman *37*
Bowling Green *21*
Broadway *21, 28, 30, 39, 44*
Bronx *8, 9*
Brooklyn *7, 8, 9, 17, 25, 26, 27, 44*
Canal Street *27, 28*
Castle Clinton National Monument *14, 15*
Central Park *6, 10, 29, 39, 40, 41, 43*
Chinatown *25, 26, 27*
Chrysler Building *33*
City Hall *13, 21, 25*
City Hall Park *13, 25*
Cloisters, The *43*
Columbia University *42, 43*
Commodities Exchange Center *22*
East River *9, 14, 24, 29, 30, 33, 35*
Ellis Island *14, 17, 18*
Empire State Building *5, 30, 31, 33*
Erie Canal *8*
F.A.O. Schwartz *37*
Federal Hall National Memorial *21*
Federal Reserve Bank *21*
Fifth Avenue *6, 28, 30, 33, 41*
Flatiron Building *13*

Fort Tryon Park *43*
Fulton Fish Market *24, 25*
Governors Island *14, 15, 19*
Grand Central Terminal *33*
Greenwich Village *28*
Guggenheim Museum *41*
Guinness World Records Exhibit Hall *33*
Hamilton, Alexander *8*
Hammarskjöld Library *35*
Harlem *41, 42, 43*
Harlem River *9*
Hayden Planetarium *41*
Hudson, Henry *6*
Hudson River *5, 8, 9, 13, 14, 28, 29, 30, 43*
Jacob K. Javits Convention Center *30*
Juilliard School of Music *40*
Lazarus, Emma *17*
Liberty Island *15, 18*
Lincoln Center for the Performing Arts *40*
Little Italy *27*
Long Island *5, 8, 27*
Lower East Side *25, 27, 42*
Madison Square Garden *30*
Metropolitan Museum of Art *41, 43*
Minuit, Peter *7*
Museum of Holography *28*
National Broadcasting Company (NBC) *36*
New York City Fire Museum *28*
New York Harbor *6, 14, 17, 19*
New York Stock Exchange *21*
New York University *28*
Pennsylvania Station *30, 31*
Queens *8, 10*
Radio City Music Hall Entertainment Center *35, 36*
Rockefeller Center *30, 35, 37*
Roosevelt Island *11, 35*
Saint Patrick's Cathedral *37*

Saks Fifth Avenue *37*
South Street Seaport *12, 22, 23, 24*
Staten Island *8, 18, 19, 44*
Staten Island Ferry *18, 19*
Statue of Liberty *5, 14, 15, 17, 18*
Times Square *30, 38, 39*
Titanic Memorial Lighthouse *24*
United Nations *5, 30, 33, 34, 35*
Wall Street *12, 19, 21*
Washington, George *7, 21, 25, 28*
Washington Square *28, 29*
Whitney Museum of American Art *33, 41*
World Trade Center *12, 21, 22*